The Oriole & the Ovenbird

The Oriole & the Ovenbird

Poems by

Angela Patten

© 2021 Angela Patten. All rights reserved.
This material may not be reproduced in any form, published,
reprinted, recorded, performed, broadcast,
rewritten or redistributed without
the explicit permission of Angela Patten.
All such actions are strictly prohibited by law.

Cover design by Shay Culligan

Cover art by Adelaide Murphy Tyrol,
Caribbean Emerald (extinct). 5" x 8" oil on board
Adelaide Murphy Tyrol is a natural history artist-illustrator
who lives and works in Vermont and New York City
(www.adelaidetyrol.com)

ISBN: 978-1-952326-91-2

Kelsay Books
502 South 1040 East, A-119
American Fork, Utah, 84003

For Daniel

Acknowledgments

Thanks to my paddling and bird-watching friends Andy Naughton, David Blanchard, Eve Pranis, Jeff Salisbury, Mary Ann Samuels and Michele Tulis for sharing their pleasure in the natural world. Thanks also to POettes Anna Blackmer, Sue Burton, Judith Chalmer and Florence McCloud for their support and feedback. Special thanks to my brother John Goggins for transportation to various bird sanctuaries around Ireland and so much more. Grants from The Vermont Arts Endowment and the University of Vermont helped support the writing of many of these poems. Finally, my thanks to the editors of the following journals where some of these poems first appeared:

Crosswinds Poetry Journal: "Spring Comes to a Dying Decade," "Tracks" *

Cumberland River Review: "Glendalough Sonnet"

Live Encounters: "Slow Time," "The Catbird," "Ever Since Breaking My Wrist," "The Thing with Feathers," "Whither the Ovenbird," "A Cacophony of Crows"

Sequestrum Journal of Literature and the Arts: "Ravens," "Crowtime"

Southlight Magazine (Scotland): "Starlings Stop Time!"

The Cafe Review: "Species-ism"

The Raven's Perch: "Blood Moon," "Drinking It In"

* Winner, *Cultural Center of Cape Cod* National Poetry Prize 2016

Contents

Tracks	11
No Laughing, No Talking, No Red Light	12
Slow Time	13
Hillwalking, Glencolmcille, County Donegal	14
After Cataract Surgery	16
After the Storm	18
Crowtime	19
Notes for a Possible Poem	21
Spring Comes to a Dying Decade	22
The Thing with Feathers	23
Species-ism	24
Starlings Stop Time!	25
Evening Light at Oakledge	27
Tides	29
Ever Since Breaking My Wrist	31
Whither the Ovenbird	32
The Catbird	33
A Cacophony of Crows	34
Drinking It In	35
Ravens	36
Glendalough Sonnet	37

Tracks

After surgery the stitch-marks
look like bird-feet walking up my arm.
But what strange bird has left
its bone-white prints
embedded in my wrist like needle-tracks?
Perhaps it was the raven
that faux-sorrowful funeral director
walking beak-forward, gloved hands
folded behind his back, who walks the
twin trajectories of a railway line
that leads to a long-defunct station
where I might meet myself returning
from the beach with two scabbed knees
embossed inoculations against disease
the weals of ancient injuries like medals
from the battlefields of childhood
and my mother's crowsfeet
inching toward my eyes.

No Laughing, No Talking, No Red Light

for Lin

Let your regrets become egrets
—Marylen Grigas

Like trying to lasso the air this effort
to reel in my attention to the water
flowing around my little boat, the blister
on my thumb from paddling, the birds
calling in unfathomable foreign languages—

the memory of all the moments
I wasted on worry and regret.

Let them fly into the busy undergrowth
where humble muskrats nibble on stalks
geese honk warnings from the sidelines
beavers slap their flat tails on the water
and a black-crowned night heron
doffs his feathered cap in my direction.

I am only looking, I tell them. Trying
to be quiet. Just keeping an eye on things.

Slow Time

A warm breeze blows through the willows
rings the wind-chime by the screen door.

I raise my head to see an emerald hummingbird
stop at the coral bells in the herb garden

then take a turn at the purple heliotrope
like a French perfumer fashioning a fragrance.

Chipmunk comes to nibble sunflower seeds
pale paws resting on my outstretched fingers.

Bees hang on the whirling butterfly bush
bending the flowers with their body weight.

A swallowtail settles on a feathery dill stalk
with the dignified etiquette of a courtesan

trained in the arts of music and calligraphy
to orchestrate a leisurely mutual seduction.

Hillwalking, Glencolmcille, County Donegal

A strip of grass running down the middle
of the road tells how rarely a car appears.
Sheep graze unfenced everywhere
raising their white startled faces at sound
of a hill-walker's jaunty whistle.

Yesterday a man with a flat slane
came to slice and stack the sods of turf
into teepees for the wind to dry
as though he were setting a fire
in his cottage hearth at home.

Now the turf has shed its brackish liquid
and each damp lump leans against its neighbor
like all the little houses standing
shoulder to shoulder in the glen.

We can see their lights come on
when the long summer evening dwindles
and we turn aside from our hillwalking
to take in the view.

It is said that years ago the locals
were wary of newfangled electricity
until a priest, still venerated in these parts
persuaded them it was a gift from God.

He led them on a journey through the village
a rushlight held aloft like a monstrance
his black cassock billowing behind.
By sleight of hand exchanged the rushes
for a candle, then a lighted torch
and finally an oil lamp.

At last by prearrangement a hidden
acolyte depressed a switch and lo!
electric light eradicated darkness.

The oldest woman in the parish
acknowledging celestial stagecraft
gave the experiment her blessing.

Looking out beyond the cliffs to the wild Atlantic
and beyond that to the rim of the world
you wonder what might have moved
that madman missionary Colmcille
to set out to sea in a wooden currach.

Did he wish himself a dove
that could fly above the waves
bearing the lighted match of faith in his beak
to set the distant lands on fire?

And what still moves his followers to wander
in his footsteps muttering Hail Marys
as they kneel before the numbered signs
to tick off each station on their pilgrimage?

Still remnants of a prehistoric past endure
whose rocks and wells and sacred stones
were worshipped long before the Christians
plastered over it with saints and statues.

Up here on the mountain there is only wind
that blows all voices—ancient, modern—
out to sea where fulmars, gulls and gannets
do not believe in any god but hunger.

After Cataract Surgery

The source of all light is in the eye.
                    —Alan Watts

My father forfeited one eye
to clerical brutality
in that country of the blind
where priests were permitted to impose
their hellish visions on the innocent
the foolish, and the weak.

Did it restore some crucial balance
in the universe when the ophthalmologist
withdrew the gauzy cataract
through a pinhole aperture
in my own blue eye like Jesus
who restored the blind man's sight
by mixing sacred spittle in the dirt?

And was it only cataract removal
that made the goldenrod more deeply yellow
when I emerged days later from
the shadowed woods into the sunlit field?

Why had I never noticed the discarded seed-pod
of the Queen Anne's Lace was a tiny basket
intricate as a bird's abandoned nest?

The Monarch on the Joe Pye Weed
opened and then closed its wings
quivering with excess of love
like a Victorian lady fluent
in the language of fans.

How many of us with two good eyes
reduce our worldview to a small rectangle
gazing at our palms like children peering
through the windows of a dollhouse?

After the Storm

Calm and sunny now, the snow
like eggwhites and sugar
whipped to a creamy sheen.

Cardinal shows up at the feeder
conscious of the dashing figure
he cuts in his ecclesiastical robe.

Catholic cardinals wear scarlet
symbol of their readiness
to shed their blood for Christ—

a gruesome faith. Cardinal
at the bird feeder might scoff
at such a bird-brained notion.

He flies in like a feathered arrow
to its target, unstoppable
as hunger, red as desire.

Crowtime

It is said that crows, like other corvids, recognize themselves in mirrors and this is thought to show intelligence.
—Scientific American

The last light of a winter's day—
thousands of winged forms
flap past my windows—pins
pulled by a powerful magnet.

The sky is black with crows
crying in cracked voices of their plans
to steal what is left of the light
to gather their feathered shapes
into a solid-color jigsaw puzzle
of land and lake and sky
that will click into place
only when the last bird
flies into its jagged aperture
and darkness falls.

Like the crows, my father
showed up night after night
to take his place in an ancient ritual.
To play his fiddle, not by standing out
but by fitting in with the other men
those dark-suited bus drivers and conductors
who brought to the session
all their quirks and oddities—
Mr. Ward with his head thrown back,
the accordion at rest on his round belly—
Mr. Keogh with his albino eyes
long fingers sawing the fiddle—
and young Tony in short trousers
tootling away on the tin whistle.

Now my father too is part of that
collective darkness, the puzzle
that the crows remake each night.
That dawn, like a wayward child,
scatters joyfully each morning.

Notes for a Possible Poem

How hard to leave the house some days
to clamber out of the declivity of self.

After days of paralysis, this reprieve.

An icy gloss has turned the snow
into the inch-thick Royal icing
on my mother's longlost Christmas cake.

Red cardinal lands by the bird-feeder
a tongue of fire in the white landscape.

I might step out to get the mail
then decide to keep walking.

I might climb the hill to Redrocks Park
to see the lake boiling like a cauldron
long plumes curling over the water's surface
then circle down through the woods
to stand close to the waves
as they dash against the rocks
to form great exoskeletons of ice.

I might jog down the salted street
to the private beach at South Cove.
Beyond the *No Trespassing* sign
the lake will loom pink as a flamingo
in late evening light.

Later we might drive off together
into the silvery landscape
your warm hand resting on my knee
all the way home.

Spring Comes to a Dying Decade

Here's the house finch with his flaming breast
the goldfinch yellowing up like a canary
the cardinal fully incarnadined. It must be Spring.

And it's as if we were back in the early Sixties
staring at the static on our tiny black-and-white TVs
eating porridge and potatoes in a muted universe

when suddenly it was all brilliant plumage. Cuffs
like ruffed grouse. Mother wore a woodpecker's
red beret. Brother was an Icterine Warbler

in a paisley cravat. Dark-suited men dared to wear
pink shirts like shy flycatchers. Even the priest risked
a raven-black leather jacket and a mood-ring.

The world turned bottoms-up like a tufted titmouse
freeloading at the feeder, raucous squawks asserting
what we instantly twigged was *Mating Season.*

The Thing with Feathers

May morning outside my study window—
two warring blue jays shake a shower
of blossoms from the apple tree.

In high summer the scarlet cardinal
adds a new phrase to his song—
the metallic twang of a mouth-harp.

Three woodpeckers circumnavigate
the walnut tree outside our house.
Red-capped adult on the highest branch.
Young ones below halt their hammering
to grouse about their parent's blithe
refusal to continue feeding them.

At birding class I learn the early Colonists
killed and studied countless shorebirds
then lovingly bestowed the familiar names
by which we know them today.

For instance, the Kildeer
used to be called a Chattering Plover.
I wonder what name he might assign
for himself and his kind?

This morning blood and feathers in the snow—
remains of a hawk's midday meal
that we unwittingly catered with our menu
of sunflower seeds and suet.

A rapacious starling at our feeder
seizes all the seeds for himself.
Yet in a murmuration of thousands
he will ascend almost to holiness.

Species-ism

A gang of noisy grackles at the feeder
bullies the small birds away.
Fierce as Vikings, they dive bomb
each other, Prussian blue heads
shimmering in the light.

Next the starlings, black feathers
cool as leather jackets
of The Jets from *West Side Story*
sporting vicious yellow beaks
like dangling cigarettes.

We who profess to love birds
abhor the grackles, starlings, jays
those raucous squawkers
scrounging peanut-studded suet
black oil sunflower and thistle seed.

No sense of decorum, restraint
or the fitness of things.

We prefer small brown flycatchers
and finches garbed in olive-grey
that daintily select a single seed
then fly away to crack it open
on a private branch.

Polite, well-behaved birds
that know their proper place
as we observe our own invisible fences
nod guarded greetings to those neighbors
who maintain the flowerbeds
but keep their distance.

Starlings Stop Time!

In 1949 the hands of Big Ben slowed by four and a half minutes after a flock of starlings perched on the minute hand.
—The Oxford Book of Birds

Likely it was only bickering
for dominance, not a proletariat plea
for better nesting conditions or
workplace safety in the face
of the despotic factory clock.

But what if one visionary starling
his breast puffed up with pride
had tried to organize the masses?

Look what humans have accomplished
with the sheer weight of numbers
he might have tweeted—
built the Transcontinental Railroad
and the Cathedral at Chartres
melted polar icecaps, hunted
the Passenger Pigeon
and the Spectacled Cormorant
even the Great Auk to extinction.

Perhaps he had heard of Gulliver
thwarted in his travels and tied down
with string by tiny Lilliputians?

How many starlings would it take
to stop the Big Clock's
minute hand from turning?

No one lifted a feather in support
busy as they were with nest building
and serial mating to ensure survival

until a shower of nestlings no doubt
in search of a higher purpose
flew up to balance on the colossal hand
their airy weight enough to tip
the 220-pound pendulum by
a fraction of an inch.

The great heart halted as if shaken
by arrhythmia so that people far below
paused, looked up and marveled
supposing that sudden stop was an act
of god or birds were angels dancing
on the head of a pin, as if they might
have learned the answer to that old chestnut
about the sound of one hand clapping.

Evening Light at Oakledge

Nothing gold can stay.
      —Robert Frost

But I love the soft gold light
of summer evenings, a slight breeze
swaying the tall grass, dark trees
nameless in the distance.

The city plans to let this meadow
return to forest to fulfill
some worthy ecological goal.

But I will mourn this horizon line
of yellow ochre hazy in the heat
purple clover underfoot
timothy and touch-me-not alive
with creatures rustling and lamenting
in their own strange languages.

Small birds dart back and forth
conducting their inscrutable errands
uttering sounds we can never translate
for all our deft mnemonics—
teacher teacher, peter peter, pretty girl

A sparkle in the corner of my eye
might be a beer-can. No matter.
I prefer the gauzy goldleaved long shot
to the unkind clarity of the close-up.

Tonight I might have stayed inside
morose, immune to wonder.
This evening's light would have shone
with or without an audience

like a poet who keeps on writing
even if no one comes to sit
on those hard folding chairs
emits inarticulate embarrassing groans
then rushes up at the end to say
she really really liked your work.

Tides

Low tide at Seapoint discloses
long stone steps and a railing
leading down to the sea.

The squat Martello tower
still guards the Irish coast.
I am a ghost visiting my childhood

unnoticed among the bathers—
hardy pensioners in ancient togs
attention-seeking teens shrieking

at shock of icy water, calling names
elbowing each other to
get in, go on, I double-dare you.

The smell a rich anthology
of rotting wrack and silica
merged with the remains

of last night's carnage
committed by the glass-eyed gulls
and oil-dark cormorants.

Ruddy turnstones wade
in the shallows like Dalits
doomed to scavenge for eternity.

Once I was part of a tangled tribe
of children, salt-water famished
clamoring for sandwiches and tea.

Low tide revealed the barnacled rocks
the stony beach we had to walk
wincing, to reach the sea.

Twice-daily alchemy of high tide
transformed the scene as though it were
a canvas overpainted by Vermeer—

at times in tiers of verdigris and indigo
the cool blue-greys of tiled interiors
or the tranquil lapis of a satin gown.

Ever Since Breaking My Wrist

I've noticed that the woodpecker
hopping from deck rail to deck rail
to reach the suet-cage, looks somehow—
armless—and the raven picking
seeds up from the snow, bright eyes
darting this way and that, appears—
vulnerable—on two spindly legs
like a prisoner in handcuffs
or a card-sharp nailed for dealing
from the middle of the deck.

It is always disarming to see a bird in flight.
The great blue heron, perched on one leg
like a battered armature, takes off
crying out his *cawchee* in disgust.

We look up from our fiberglas canoe
to see him suddenly become sprung
rhythm, great wings beating the wind
in a slow disdainful dance.

John James Audubon loved birds so much
he sometimes killed a dozen before finding
the perfect model, then pinned it down with wires
to create a lifelike image of a bird in flight.

And though my Kevlar-covered broken wing
will heal in time, I still rejoice that birds
can take their leave of us without regret
by pulling the ace of flying from their sleeves.

Whither the Ovenbird

Because I too come from
a long line of nobodies
and he is a small warbler
with insistent voice
and inconspicuous plumage.

His song rings out in summer
hardwood forests—
teacher-teacher-teacher—
as if imploring academics
to lay down their dusty books
their medieval regalia.

The ovenbird has no time
for such artifice.
His olive-brown feathers
spotted breast and rufous crown
blend with the woodland palette—
tawny soil, peaty sod
grey green of mosses
autumnal camouflage.

Extravagantly creative
yet practical as bread
the ovenbird builds a leafy dome
like a Quebeçois clay oven
part of his elaborate courtship ritual
his industry an open invitation—

come join me in my humble labor
and help leaven it with song.

The Catbird

What good is it, this constant tweeting
bleating, weeping in the languages of others
as if it longed to be a different kind of bird?

Perhaps a yellow-bellied sapsucker
whose drumming sounds like stuttering cadence
of a wartime message in Morse Code?

Or a goldfinch warbling in his courting colors?
Or any one of those pitch-perfect passerines
so self-possessed, so poised at public speaking?

I don't fit in, the catbird seems to cry. This
series of impressions, this stand-up comedy routine
these whistles, squeaks and gurgles are not

a territorial device. Neither are they mockery.
A secret: I am not contented in this costume.
I never liked my given song. Hidden in the bushes

I listen to your myriad inflections, riffs and jingles
like an operatic understudy rehearsing in the wings
waiting for my cue to join the choir.

A Cacophony of Crows

At dusk all the crows in our neighborhood
gather in the tallest pines
like old men in tarnished suits
meeting for *unhappy hour.*

The sky is full of their feathered shapes
their tattered vestments. The air
thick with their raucous talk
their carping discordant music.

Why now as the day wanes
do they gather by the thousand
as if to bear witness to the sun
slipping like a stone
into the glinting lake?

The scientist calls their gathering
a *flock,* the poet a *murder.*

Our communal roosts are condominiums
whose size and situation
indicate our place in the pecking order.
Stretching away to the horizon
supplanting woodlands, cornfields
farms and kitchen gardens
they keep us safe from predators
close to food sources, social amenities.

At dusk the cacophony of crows
drags us out of our dwellings
to stand, flightless as rails
staring upwards at the juddering trees.

Drinking It In

for Eve

Writing a poem is one of the ways to love the world.
—Stephen Dobyns

The hummingbird, dressed for dinner
in ruby cravat and emerald tuxedo
samples first the red, then yellow
then the purple flowers, their colors
throbbing in the heat of August.

Does it matter that I've lost their names?
Botany is a science after all
and my careful schoolgirl drawings
of pistil, sepal, stamen
were full of right-brain love
not evidence of scientific literacy.

This bird—sommelier of summer's wine
connoisseur of color, tiny rocket
wind-up toy—cares nothing for taxonomy
who won last night's state senate race
nor who will be elected president
in November when summer is no more.

This one-ounce wonder
aerial *artiste* now hovering mid-air
on a flying trapeze of whirring wings
cares only for the botany of desire.

Each bloom deflowered
with hypodermic accuracy.
Each little death a metaphor
needing no further analysis.

Ravens

In Norse mythology the twin ravens
Thought and Memory, flew about
the world, collecting news for Odin
who had given them the gift of speech.

Did they work together as a team—
one forward-thinking, looking out
for bloody rumor, thin whisper
foul-smelling allegation, while the other
mouthed words and phrases
recited names, reiterated everything?

Did they return together, grigged
with gossip for the dinner table?
Or did Thought sometimes muddle
Memory with unanswerable questions—
Can Memory be trusted?
Does Thought delude itself?
Do we only live as long as Memory
wraps us in its wings?

Odin feared they might not return
knowing their taste for decomposing flesh
what that vertiginous perspective
might reveal—a new god with a dove
that whispers in his ear, some new
dark truth delivered from the air.

Glendalough Sonnet

for Martin

Rain and relatives, relatives and rain.
In Glendalough's monastic town
a jackdaw baby thrusts his downy head
out of a round tower *putlock* and raises
an ungodly yellow beak to squawk
at gawking tourists snapping cellphones
the spines of their umbrellas dripping
on the ancient *bullaun* stones
where monks once mixed their potions
and the holy well was rich in lithium
which turned out to be a great cure
for the occasional pilgrim who, like me
suffered from the watery weather
or a sodden slough of Celtic despond.

About the Author

Angela Patten's publications include three poetry collections, *In Praise of Usefulness* (Wind Ridge Books), *Reliquaries* and *Still Listening* (Salmon Poetry, Ireland), and a prose memoir, *High Tea at a Low Table: Stories From An Irish Childhood* (Wind Ridge Books). Her work has appeared in many literary journals and anthologies. Born and raised in Dublin, Ireland, she now lives in Burlington, Vermont, where she is a Senior Lecturer in the University of Vermont English Department.

Kelsay Books

www.ingramcontent.com/pod-product-compliance
Lightning Source LLC
Chambersburg PA
CBHW071642090426
42738CB00013B/3185